Kief Preston's Time-Tested Edibles Cookbook:

Medical Marijuana Recipes

-CANNABUTTER EDITION-

by Kief Preston

© 2016

COPYRIGHT

TABLE OF CONTENTS

COPYRIGHT   2

INTRODUCTION   5

EXTRACTION   7

CANNABIS-CRISPY-TREATS   12

CECI'S-CANNADIAN-CANNA-PECAN-PIE   14

CHOCOLATE-NUT-CANNA-BITES   17

CITRUS-CANNA-BREAD   20

COCOA-CANNA-POUND-CAKE   24

GANJA-PEANUT-BUTTER-COOKIES   27

ROLLING-STONER-STONES   31

POT-PUPPY-CHOW   34

POT-WINGS   37

SUPER-STONER-CUPCAKES   40

FIRE-FRENCH-TOAST   44

CANNALICIOUS-FUDGE   47

PEANUT-TOFFEE-POT-CORN   51

CANNABUTTER-BISCUITS   55

MARY'S-MASHED-POT-TATOES   58

BUD-BROCCOLI-CASSAROLE   61

CHEESY-MACCARONI-N-TREEZ   64

GET-HIGH-STIR-FRY   68

CHOCOLATE-CHIP-CANNABUTTER-BARS 72

CHICKEN-POT-PIE   75

SMOKIN'-SMORES   79

CONCLUSION   83

THE KIEF PRESTON'S TIME TESTED
EDIBLES COOKBOOK SERIES   86

BEFORE YOU GO   89

YOUR BONUS   90

DISCLAMER   92

INTRODUCTION

High there! Do you enjoy mouth-watering edible THC deliciousness and want to prepare it yourself? Kief Preston here, and I bet you do! Having been a medical marijuana patient for years now, I have come across my fair share of suuuper tasty (as well as some not so tasty) edibles. I have also been collecting and preparing a bunch of different medical edible recipes myself, especially those that were both delicious and easy to understand. Some of them were so bomb that I felt I needed to share them with my fellow medical marijuana patients and anyone else who is legally allowed to consume cannabis containing products. I recently went back to an old notebook that I've been keeping and jotting down recipes in, and picked out my all-time most favorite recipes EVER, guaranteed to satiate your appetite and make you feel fantastic! I posted up in front of my computer with a jar of Bubba Kush and put them all together in convenient e-book format for all you hungry cannabis consumers out there. Some of these recipes I tried in Europe, others are from the United States. But all are absolutely delicious and also easy enough to follow, even if you've already taken your medicine today. I suggest sticking to the script the first time, and add you own twist and modify any of the recipes as desired the next time around. Also, don't forget to check out the conclusion to find out how to get my *Kief Preston's Time-Tested Edibles Cookbook: Coconut Oil Edition* absolutely FREE!   -Kief

EXTRACTION

As you probably already know, you can't just eat marijuana straight-up. You will need to extract the THC, the main psychoactive ingredient and decarboxylate it. The most common way to do this is to make a cannabis-infused butter-based substance commonly referred to by the world as "cannabutter". All of the irresistible recipes found in this book require the use of cannabutter (*Cooking With Kief Edition* coming soon). My favorite way to make cannabutter is described below, for more extraction tips, including another cannabutter recipe and how to decarboxylate your meds, please visit KiefPreston.com and click "Resources" on the homepage or in Kief's Weed

Blog. So lets get started making some bomb and **hella potent** cannabutter right now!

You will need:

4 sticks of butter (1 LB) – can be salted or not

1-1.5 OZ of medicine

1 mesh strainer

1 cheesecloth

1 spoon or fork

1 small crockpot (any small sized pot will work)

1 grinder (optional)

1 food processor (optional)

Directions:

- Grind your medicine as finely as possible with grinder or a food processor if you happen to have one around.

- Combine the medicine and butter in the crockpot. Set it on low (between 200 degrees and 220 degrees Fahrenheit). Most of the small ones only have one operating temperature, which works great. If using a pot on the stove, keep the heat LOW - MEDIUM taking care not to burn the butter.

- Stir until butter is melted and incorporated with your medicine.

- Cover with a lid, and leave it to simmer for 6 hours. This eliminates the need for decarboxylation because you are giving the herb enough time to decarb during the extraction process already. Slow and low is the way to go, trust me! If you are absolutely unable to wait that long, give it at least 4, keeping in mind you might be leaving some THC behind. You can also try the faster cannabutter recipe described in the video on in the "Resources" section of <u>KiefPreston.com</u>.

• Next, turn off your crockpot and strain your butter mixture through a cheesecloth over a mesh strainer, into a brownie pan or something similar, preferably pyrex. Make sure to give it a good squeeze or two!

• Let it cool to room temperature and cover it. You are now ready to start cooking with cannabis!

• Place any unused portion in the fridge.

- If you want to make less, you can always just use half of everything, as long as you make sure to let it simmer for the same amount of time.

- ENJOY!

For help converting cups, teaspoons, ounces, pounds, grams or whatever pleas go to:

http://www.traditionaloven.com/conversions_of_m easures/butter_converter.html

CANNABIS-CRISPY-TREATS

Ingredients:

2/3 of a stick of cannabutter

1 x 10 ounce bag of regular or mini marshmallows

6 cups of crispy rice cereal of your choice

1 x 12 ounce package of butterscotch chips

You will also need:

1 baking pan (13"x 9"x 2"suggested)

1 saucepan

Directions:

- Melt the cannabutter in a large saucepan over low heat.
- Add marshmallows and mix until completely melted and then remove from heat.
- Immediately add the cereal and stir until coated.
- Mix in the butterscotch chips.
- Press the mixture into a greased 13"x 9"x 2" baking pan.
- Let it chill until the mixture hardens a bit. Cut into 2-inch squares.
- The potency of the treats can be adjusted by cutting bigger squares (3-inch suggested).
- ENJOY!

CECI'S-CANNADIAN-CANNA-PECAN-PIE

Ingredients:

3 tablespoons of extra strong cannabutter,

3 beaten eggs,

3/4 cup of brown sugar

2 tablespoons of flour

1 teaspoon of vanilla extract

3/4 cup of corn syrup

3 tablespoons of bourbon liquor (whiskey)

1½ cups of pecans

1/2 cup of milk chocolate chips

1 x 9 inch unbaked pie shell.

You will also need:

1 bowl

1 saucepan

Directions:

- First thing you want to do is preheat your oven to 350 degrees Fahrenheit.
- Next, put your cannabutter in a saucepan and melt it down.
- Take your eggs and place them in a bowl and then slowly stir in your brown sugar, vanilla, corn syrup, and bourbon until they are well combined.
- Now add now in your melted cannabutter and stir well.

- Mix in your pecans and chocolate chips. Make sure you mix it well so they are evenly distributed throughout.

- Next, take all of your ingredients and place them in your 9 inch pie shell.

- Bake at 350 degrees F for one hour (SET AN ALARM YOU CAN HEAR!)

- Now pull the pie out of the oven and let it cool for e few minutes.

- ENJOY!

CHOCOLATE-NUT-CANNA-BITES

Ingredients:

2½ cups of milk chocolate chips

1/2 cup (1 stick) of cannabutter

4 cups of large marshmallows cut in half

1 cup of unsalted roasted peanuts

1/2 cup of toasted coconut

1/2 cup of glazed cherries

You will also need:

1 aluminum baking pan (8"x 8"suggested)

1 microwave safe bowl

Directions:

- Grease the aluminum baking pan with about 1 tablespoon of cannabutter.
- Set the rest aside and leave it for the later.
- Place chocolate into a large microwave safe bowl and heat on medium heat for 30 second intervals, stirring until melted.
- Combine the rest of the cannabutter with the melted chocolate.
- Microwave for 15 seconds or until the cannabutter is fully melted and stir into the chocolate.
- Stir until both are well mixed.
- Now pour in the marshmallows, peanuts, coconut and glazed cherries.
- Mix everything together.

- Pour into the baking pan and chill in fridge until firm.

- Now you are ready to cut your squares, serve'em

- ENJOY!

CITRUS-CANNA-BREAD

Ingredients:

1 stick cannabutter (equal to 1/2 cup or 1/4 LB)

1.5 cups flour

1.5 cups cane sugar

2 large eggs

1/2 cup milk

1/2 cups chopped walnuts

1 juiced lemon (or ½ juiced orange)

1 tsp. lemon zest (again orange works great too)

1 tsp. baking powder

1/2 tsp. salt

You will also need:

1 baking pan (9"x 5"suggested)

1 bowl

Directions:

- Preheat your oven to 350 degrees Fahrenheit.
- In a small bowl, mix the flour, salt (or lemon salt) and baking powder, until blended thoroughly.
- In a separate but larger bowl, mix the softened cannabutter, eggs and cup of sugar together.
- Next add the milk and flour, first adding milk, then flour, then milk and then flour.
- Blend all of this this thoroughly.

- Now mix in the lemon zest, followed by the walnuts nuts.

- Pour this mixture into a buttered and floured 9" x 5" baking pan.

- Place this in the oven for 60 minutes (preheated to 350F). MAKE SURE TO SET A TIMER YOU CAN HEAR! This is the part when I usually roll a cone.

- After an hour, take it out and let it cool a few minutes before you take it out of the pan.

- Now that the baking process is finished and your delicious and fragrant Citrus-Canna-Bread is cooling, mix the remaining ½ cup cane sugar and the lemon juice (from one lemon) thoroughly, until it becomes a lightly syrupy consistency and use this as a glaze.

- Pour over the cooled bread and let it dry. Or if you can't wait any longer just cut a piece and dig in!

- You can also try swapping out the lemon for a small orange to change it up!

- ENJOY!

COCOA-CANNA-POUND-CAKE

Ingredients:

1 cup of cannabutter (1/2 LB)

3 cups of cane sugar

3 cups flour

1/2 cup shortening

5 medium eggs

5 tbsp. cocoa powder

1 cup of milk

1 tsp. vanilla extract

1/2 tsp. table salt

1/2 tsp. baking powder (not soda)

You will also need:

1 large bowl

1 pound cake pan (10"suggested)

Directions:

- First, preheat the oven to 325 degrees Fahrenheit.
- Get out a large mixing bowl and beat together the shortening and the cannabis butter, subsequently adding the cane sugar, mixing thoroughly.
- Now add the eggs one at a time, mixing well after each egg.
- Next beat in the vanilla.

- In a separate bowl, combine the dry ingredients and add to the first mixing bowl, switching off each addition with a little milk.

- Stir after each addition.

- Get out a 10" tube pan (pound cake pan), grease or butter the pan and place it in the oven for about 80 minutes. MAKE SURE YOU SET A TIMER YOU CAN HEAR!

- Finally, take your pound cake out of the oven and let it cool for 5 minutes.

- Cut into slices.

- ENJOY!

GANJA-PEANUT-BUTTER-COOKIES

Ingredients:

1 cup of cannabutter

1 cup of peanut butter

2 cups of sugar

1 cup of brown sugar

2 eggs

1 teaspoon of baking soda

1 teaspoon of baking powder

2 teaspoons of vanilla extract

2½ cups of flour

You will also need:

1 baking sheet (standard size)

2 medium or large bowls

Directions:

•   First, preheat the oven to about 365 degrees Fahrenheit.

•   Next, place the cannabutter in the microwave and melt it for about 35-50 seconds. Make sure not to boil it though.

•   Mix the melted cannabutter with one cup of peanut butter and add the one and one fourth cup of flour.

•   Now add one cup of sugar, brown sugar, the eggs, baking soda, baking powder and vanilla.

- At this point, you can add the remaining flour.

- Place the remaining 1 cup of sugar in a separate bowl.

- Get a spoon and mold the cookies into balls that can fit easily in the palm of your hand.

- Roll cookies in the sugar and put them on an ungreased cookie sheet.

- Put them in the oven and bake for 7 – 10 minutes.

- At this point you can judge for yourself if they need another minute or two, but don't leave them in there much longer then that.

- Remove the cookies from the hot sheet and transfer them to a cool plate.

- Let them cool for a minute or enjoy them hot!

- This recipe makes about a dozen killer cookies.

- ENJOY!

ROLLING-STONER-STONES

Ingredients:

1.5 cups of cannabutter (equals 3 sticks)

3 cups of rolled oats or granola

1/4 cup of peanut butter (chunky recommended)

3 tbsp. honey

2 tbsp. cocoa powder or syrup

You will also need:

1 medium saucepan

1 glass baking pan

1 ice cream scoop

1 tupperware container (optional)

Directions:

- In a medium saucepan melt the cannabutter over low heat.
- Add all the other ingredients, stirring until well mixed.
- Cook an additional 2 - 3 minutes over medium low heat, stirring continuously.
- Spread mixture into glass baking pan and place in the freezer for 10 - 15 minutes.
- Take out of freezer and form into balls with an ice cream scoop.
- Place on wax paper in a plastic container and keep in refrigerator.
- Warning: Inexperienced users should eat 1/2 a stoner-stone and see how they feel, before consuming more!!! They may look hella harmless,

but as you probably already know, when it comes to medical marijuana edibles, looks can be very deceiving.

- ENJOY!

POT-PUPPY-CHOW

Ingredients:

6 cups of any variety of Chex or similar type of cereal

1/2 cup of dried banana chips (only if you like bananas)

3/4 cup of semi sweet chocolate chips

1/3 cup of peanut butter

1/4 cup of cannabutter

1/2 tsp of vanilla extract

1 cup of powdered sugar

You will also need:

2 large bowls (at least one microwavable)

Large Zip-lock type plastic bag

Directions:

- In a large bowl, measure and combine your cereal and banana chips.
- Set that bowl aside.
- In another large but microwaveable bowl, microwave the chocolate and peanut butter until melted.
- Check every 30 seconds.
- Now, stir in your vanilla and melted, or room temperature cannabutter. Do not microwave the cannabutter!

- Pour this chocolaty mixture over the cereal/banana mixture and stir until coated.

- Place contents in a large Zip-lock type bag.

- Now add powdered sugar to the bag and shake vigorously until most pieces of cereal and bananas are evenly coated.

- Divide into 7 servings.

- ENJOY!

POT-WINGS

Ingredients:

25 chicken wings

1/2 cup of cannabutter, melted

6 ounces of tomato sauce, canned will work

1/2 cup of red hot-sauce like Tabasco

1 teaspoon of chili powder

1 teaspoon of garlic powder

You will also need:

1 baking sheet (standard size)

1 large bowl

Directions:

- Preheat your oven to 400 degrees F.

- Place plain wings in the oven and bake them for 25 minutes, or until cooked through/to your liking.

- Next, melt your cannabutter in the microwave and combine it with the hot sauce, the tomato sauce, the garlic and chili powder in your large bowl.

- Mix and toss the cooked wings in the sauce mixture a few times, making sure to coat them relatively well and covering each wing with about the same amount of sauce.

- Return the coated wings to your baking sheet.

- Reduce oven to 250 and bake for another 20 minutes.

- Next, take them out of the oven.

- Let them cool for about 5 minutes and serve.

- ENJOY!

SUPER-STONER-CUPCAKES

Ingredients:

Cupcakes

1 tablespoon less than 1¾ cups of all-purpose flour

1/2 a teaspoon of salt

1¾ teaspoons of baking powder

1 cup of granulated sugar

1/2 cup of Crisco

1/2 cup of cannabutter, at room temperature

2 eggs

1/2 a cup of milk

1/2 teaspoon of vanilla extract

1/2 teaspoon of lemon extract

Frosting

1 Betty Crocker Rich and Creamy fluffy white frosting is recommended but feel free to substitute your favorite kind and you can even add sprinkles if you fell like it! For maximum potency, and if you think you can handle it, I suggest using the *Canilla-Cream-Cheese-Frosting* recipe from **Kief Preston's Time-Tested Fastest Edibles Cookbook.**

You will also need:

2 large bowls

cupcake pans

Directions:

- First, reheat oven to 350°F.

- You should start with the cupcakes, so mix together the flour, baking powder and salt in a large bowl.

- Set this aside for later.

- Now, in another large bowl, mix the sugar with Crisco and cannabutter.

- Add the eggs, milk, vanilla, lemon extract, and the flour mixture one at a time.

- Next, mix everything together thoroughly after each ingredient is added so that you end up with a nice smooth consistency once everything has mixed in.

- Grease and flour your cupcake pans before filling three-quarters full with cake batter.

- Bake for 1 hour. MAKE SURE YOU SET A TIMER YOU CAN HEAR!

- Let the cupcakes cool before you begin frosting!

- Once they are cool, frost the cupcakes.

- ENJOY!

FIRE-FRENCH-TOAST

Ingredients:

1½ cups of heavy cream

4 eggs

1 pinch of salt

3 teaspoons of sugar

1 teaspoon of cinnamon

1/2 teaspoon of nutmeg

8 teaspoons of cannabutter (for cooking)

2 -3 more tablespoons of cannabutter (for serving, or you can use regular butter)

12 slices of your favorite bread (I use Texas-toast)

Your favorite syrup (maple, vanilla, etc...)

You will also need:

1 dish or bowl

1 large skillet

Directions:

- In a shallow dish, whisk together the eggnog, eggs, cinnamon, salt, sugar, and nutmeg and set aside.

- Melt 4 teaspoons of cannabutter in a large skillet over medium heat.

- Dredge each piece of bread in the eggnog mixture, about 15 seconds for each side.

- Then, fry the bread in the melted cannabutter, piece by piece, until golden brown on each side.

- As the bread soaks up the cannabutter, add more for each batch, teaspoon by teaspoon.

- Serve with additional cannabutter (or regular butter if you so choose) and your favorite syrup.

- ENJOY!

CANNALICIOUS-FUDGE

This one is a little more tedious to make but it tastes sooo good, so I had to add it to my all-time favorite recipes and put it in the book! Besides the usual, pot, pan, saucepan, you will also need a thermometer that goes up to about 250 degrees Fahrenheit and a wooden spoon.

Ingredients:

3 tablespoon of cannabutter

1/2 a stick of regular butter

2¾ cups of sugar

4 oz. of unsweetened chocolate

1 cup of half-and-half

1 tbsp. of corn syrup

1 tablespoons of vanilla extract

1 cup of chopped walnuts

Directions:

- First get out an 8 x 8 inch pan (or closest size you have) and grease it with the cannabis-free butter.
- Next, in a saucepan, mix together the cane sugar, chocolate pieces, half-and-half, corn syrup and your 1½ tablespoons of the cannabutter.
- Turn burner on medium and begin stirring with a wooden spoon.
- Continue stirring until the chocolate has melted and the sugar has dissolved into the chocolate.

- After this is done increase the heat just a notch above medium.

- Bring to a LOW boil.

- After it comes to a low boil, reduce the heat to medium-low, cover and boil for an additional 2 to 3 minutes.

- Next remove the cover and attach a thermometer to the pot.

- Once it reaches a temperature of 234 degrees Fahrenheit, remove from heat and add the remaining 1½ tablespoons of cannabutter. THIS IS VERY IMPORTANT

- Now just let the butter sit in the mixture and allow it to cool for 8 to 10 minutes.

- Add your vanilla and nuts, mixing thoroughly.

- Pour into the pre-greased pan and allow it to harden.

- When it has cooled and hardened, cut a square of desired size, eat it and see how you feel – make sure you wait at least an hour. Then decide how you big or how small you want to cut the rest of the portions.

- ENJOY!

PEANUT-TOFFEE-POT-CORN

Ingredients:

1 tablespoon of regular canola oil

1/4 cup of popcorn kernels (6 to 7 cups popped)

1/2 a cup of unsalted cannabutter

3/4 cup of dark brown sugar

1/2 a teaspoon Kosher salt

2 tablespoons of corn syrup

1/4 cup of maple syrup

1 cup of roasted, salted peanuts

1 teaspoon of flake salt or smoked flake salt

You will also need:

1 pot with a lid

1 medium saucepan

1 large bowl

1 baking sheet

Parchment paper

Directions:

• Place the oil and popcorn in a large pot and cover with a lid.

• Put on the stove over medium-high heat.

• Shake the pot occasionally over the burner until the popping mostly subsides, about 2 seconds between pops.

• Now pour the popcorn into a very large bowl.

- Preheat your oven to 250° Fahrenheit.

- Line a baking sheet with parchment paper.

- In a medium saucepan over medium-high heat, melt the cannabutter with the brown sugar, salt, corn syrup, and maple syrup and bring to a boil.

- GENTLY boil for 5 minutes, stirring occasionally.

- Next, add the peanuts to the mixture and then drizzle it over the popcorn.

- Stir carefully to evenly coat the popcorn.

- Now spread the coated popcorn onto the prepared baking sheet and bake for 1 hour, stirring and rotating the pan halfway through. MAKE SURE YOU SET A TIMER THAT YOU CAN HEAR!

- After an hour, pull the baking sheet out of the oven and sprinkle the popcorn with the flake salt to finish.

- Lastly, let it cool to room temperature.

- Store in an airtight container once thoroughly cooled.

- Makes enough for 4 people.

- ENJOY!

CANNABUTTER-BISCUITS

Ingredients:

2/3 cup of canna butter at room temperature

1/2 a cup of caster sugar (you can use regular

sugar, just grind it finely in a blender)

1/2 a teaspoon of vanilla extract

1 egg at room temperature

2 cups of regular white flour

1 teaspoon of baking powder

1 tablespoon of regular milk

You will also need:

1 bowl

Parchment paper

1 electric mixer

1 or 2 baking sheets (depending on size)

1 blender (optional, only needed if you want to fine-grind your sugar to make your own caster sugar)

Directions:

- First you want to preheat your oven to 355 Fahrenheit.
- Next line your baking tray(s) with parchment paper.
- Using your mixer, beat the cannabutter, sugar and vanilla in a bowl until the mixture becomes pale and creamy.
- Now add the egg and mix well.

- Next you want to sift your baking powder and flour over your butter mixture.

- Add your milk and stir everything until just combined.

- Using 1 heaping tablespoon at a time, roll mixture into ball.

- Place on the baking trays that you lined with parchment paper earlier.

- Using your tablespoon or the palm of your hand flatten the biscuits to about a half-inch thick.

- Put the baking sheets in the oven for 10 minutes, or until the biscuits turn golden brown.

- Finally pull them out of the oven and let them cool for a few minutes.

- Place them on a plate or platter to allow them to cool completely.

- ENJOY!

MARY'S-MASHED-POT-TATOES

Ingredients:

3 pounds of Yukon Gold potatoes

1 cup of low-sodium chicken broth

1 stick of cannabutter in small pieces salt

2 pinches of salt

2 inches of pepper

You will also need:

1 large pot

1 colander

1 potato riser (optional, you can always just mash

them with a fork or a potato masher instead)

Directions:

• First, you want to rinse and peel your potatoes and place them into your large pot.

• Next, add enough water so that the potatoes are covered my about 2 inches of it.

• Bring the water to a boil on high heat.

• Once it starts to boil you should reduce the heat to medium-low and simmer the potatoes uncovered for about 20 minutes.

• The potatoes should now be tender and beginning to fall apart. At this point you can drain the potatoes in your colander and let them chill for 5 minutes.

• While they are chilling, combine your broth and cannabutter in the pot you were using earlier and using medium heat, heat the mixture until the butter is well melted and hot.

• Remove the pot from the burner and season the contents with freshly ground pepper and salt according to your personal preference.

• Now take your cooked potatoes and pass them through your potato ricer into the broth/butter mixture in the pot (or you can mash them first using a fork or masher and then reintroduce to the pot).

• FOLD the potatoes and broth/butter together gently until smooth, but don't overdo it.

• Add seasoning to taste.

• ENJOY!

BUD-BROCCOLI-CASSAROLE

Ingredients:

1/2 cup of cannabutter

Vegetable oil for greasing

Florets from 2 heads of fresh broccoli (chopped)

3 cups of cooked rice

1 pound of shredded Cheddar cheese

1 cup of chopped yellow onion

1 cup of chopped celery

3 cloves garlic, (finely chopped)

1 cup of baby portabella mushrooms, (sliced)

1/4 cup of slivered almonds

1 x 10.5-ounce can of mushroom soup

1/2 a cup of day-old bread (cut into cubes)

You will also need:

1 skillet

1 baking pan (9"x 13")

1 bowl

Directions:

• Preheat your oven to 350°Farenheit.

• Melt your cannabutter in a skillet over medium heat, then remove and set aside.

• Grease a 9 x 13-inch baking pan with the vegetable oil.

• Combine the broccoli, rice, cheese, onion, celery, garlic, mushrooms, almonds, and mushroom soup in a bowl and pour them all into the baking pan.

- Soak the bread cubes in the butter, and then spread them over the entire mixture.

- Bake for 45 to 60 minutes, or until golden brown and bubbling.

- Take it out of the oven and serve.

- ENJOY!

CHEESY-MACCARONI-N-TREEZ

Ingredients:

1/2 cup of cold cannabutter

1 tablespoon of melted cannabutter

1/2 cup of regular unsalted butter

1 cup of flour

4 cups of milk

2 teaspoons of salt

1/4 teaspoon of cayenne pepper

1 teaspoon of ground black pepper

1 pound of penne pasta

1 cup of shredded smoked mozzarella cheese

1 cup of shredded Cheddar cheese

1 cup of shredded American or Swiss cheese

¾ cup of grated Parmesan cheese

¼ cup of breadcrumbs

You will also need:

1 large pot

2 medium pots

1 whisk

1 baking pan (9"x 13")

Directions:

- Preheat your oven to 350° Fahrenheit.
- Cook the penne noodles in one of the medium pots according to the label then drain and rinse under cold water and set aside.

- In a large pot over medium heat, melt the cannabutter and butter together.

- Add the flour and whisk well for 3 to 5 minutes while the mixture cooks.

- Meanwhile, in a medium pot over high heat, bring the milk just to a boil.

- Immediately after it starts to boil, slowly add the heated milk to the butter-flour mixture, whisking to incorporate well.

- Now add the salt, the cayenne and black pepper, and continue to cook until the mixture reaches a boil.

- Remove from the heat, stir in the cooked penne and cheeses, saving 1/4 cup of Parmesan cheese for the topping.

- Pour the penne mixture into a greased 9-by-13-inch baking pan.

- Combine the breadcrumbs with the remaining Parmesan and the 1 tablespoon melted cannabutter and sprinkle on top of the penne.
- Now put it in the oven and bake 30 to 40 minutes until golden brown and bubbling.
- Carefully take out of the oven and you are ready to eat.
- ENJOY!

GET-HIGH-STIR-FRY

Ingredients:

8 ounces of rice noodles

1 pork tenderloin (3/4 pound cut into 1/4-inch-thick strips)

Kosher salt

Pepper (freshly ground recommended)

3 tablespoons of cornstarch

2 cups of fat-free low-sodium chicken broth

4 teaspoons of cannabutter

4 scallions, sliced (separate the green from the white parts)

1 x 2-inch piece of ginger root (peeled and minced)

2 cloves garlic, (minced)

3 cups precut stir-fry vegetables (about 9 ounces)

Lime zest from 1 lime (keep the lime wedges for later)

You will also need:

1 large non-stick skillet

2-3 bowls

Directions:

• Cook the noodles as the label directs, then drain and rinse under cold water.

• Meanwhile, toss the pork with ¼ teaspoon of salt, pepper to taste, and 2 tablespoons of cornstarch in a bowl.

- Whisk the chicken broth and the remaining 1 tablespoon cornstarch in another bowl.

- Heat a large nonstick skillet over high heat.

- Add 1 teaspoon of cannabutter, then add the pork and stir-fry until lightly browned, about 5 minutes.

- Now transfer to a bowl.

- Add the remaining 3 teaspoons of cannabutter to the skillet, then add the scallion whites, ginger and garlic.

- Next, reduce the heat to medium and cook, stirring occasionally for about 2 minutes.

- Stir in the vegetables and 3 tablespoons water and cook, stirring occasionally, until the vegetables are crisp-tender, about 4 minutes.

- Add the broth mixture to the pan and bring it to a boil.

- Cook for about 5 minutes, stirring occasionally, until slightly thickened.

- Now return the pork to the skillet along with the noodles, lime zest and a 1/4 teaspoon of salt and stir to heat through.

- Stir in the scallion greens. Divide among bowls and serve with lime wedges.

- ENJOY!

CHOCOLATE-CHIP-CANNABUTTER-BARS

Ingredients:

1/3 cups of cannabutter

1/4 cup of honey

1/3 cup of packed brown sugar

2 cups of quick cooking oats (rolled oats don't work well)

1 cup of crispy rice cereal

1/2 teaspoon of vanilla extract

2-3 tablespoons of mini chocolate chips

You will also need:

1 large bowl

1 small pot

1 brownie pan (8"x 12")

Directions:

- In a large bowl, stir together your oats and rice cereal and set aside.
- In a small pot, melt butter, honey and brown sugar together over medium high heat until it comes to a bubble.
- Reduce the heat and cook for 2 minutes.
- Pour in the vanilla and stir.
- Now pour the mixture over dry ingredients and mix well to moisten all ingredients.

- Pour everything into a lightly greased small 8"x 12"brownie pan and press out so that the mixture in the pan is about 3/4 inch in thickness.

- Next, sprinkle the mini chocolate chips on top and press down lightly.

- Let everything cool to room temperature for about two hours or until the chocolate chips are set before cutting into bars.

- Cut, wrap in parchment paper or plastic wrap, and store at room temperature in a cool dry place.

- ENJOY!

CHICKEN-POT-PIE

Ingredients:

1 pound of skinless, boneless chicken breast halves (cubed)

1 cup of sliced carrots

1 cup of frozen green peas

1/2 cup of sliced celery

1/3 cup of cannabutter

1/3 cup of chopped onions

1/3 cup of all-purpose flour

1/2 teaspoon of salt

1/4 teaspoon of black pepper

1/4 teaspoon of celery seed

1¾ cups of chicken broth

2/3 cup of milk

2 unbaked pie crusts (9-inch)

You will also need:

1 saucepan

1 bowl

Directions:

- Preheat oven to 425 degrees Fahrenheit.
- In a saucepan, combine chicken, carrots, peas, and celery.
- Add water to cover and boil for 15 minutes.
- Remove from heat, drain and set aside.
- In the saucepan over medium heat, cook onions in Cannabutter until soft and translucent.

- Stir in your flour, salt, pepper, and celery seed.

- Slowly stir in the chicken broth and milk.

- Simmer over medium-low heat until thick.

- Now remove from heat and set aside.

- Place the chicken mixture in the bottom pie-crust.

- Pour hot liquid mixture over it and cover with the other (top) pie crust.

- Seal the edges and cut away any excess dough.

- Make several slits in the top to allow steam to escape.

- Bake in the preheated oven for about 30-35 minutes, or until pastry is golden brown and filling is bubbly.

- Pull out of the oven

- Let cool for 10 minutes

- ENJOY

SMOKIN'-SMORES

Ingredients:

7 whole graham crackers (1 cup finely crushed)

1/4 cup of powdered sugar

6 tablespoons of cannabutter (melted)

4 bars of milk chocolate candy (1.5 oz each, divided into 4)

12 large marshmallows

You will also need:

1 large Zip-loc type plastic bag

1 mini muffin tin

1 pair of kitchen shears

1 small microwave-safe bowl

Directions:

• Preheat your oven to 350 degrees Fahrenheit.

• Place the graham crackers into a large re-sealable plastic bag.

• Crush the crackers into fine crumbs.

• Now combine your graham cracker crumbs, powdered sugar, and cannabutter in a small bowl.

• Place 1 tablespoon of the crumb mixture in each cup of a mini muffin tin.

• Press crumbs into the bottom to form shallow cups.

• Bake for 4-5 minutes or until the edges start bubbling.

- In the meantime, break two of the candy bars into rectangles.

- Remove your muffin tin from the oven.

- Place one rectangle of chocolate into each cup.

- Cut the marshmallows in half crosswise using shears dipped in cold water.

- Next, put half a marshmallow, cut-side down, into each cup. Return to the oven for about 1-2 minutes or until marshmallows are slightly softened.

- Now, remove pans from oven and place on your cooling rack for about 15 minutes.

- Carefully remove the cups from the pan.

- Cool to room temperature.

- Break remaining candy bars and place in small microwavable bowl.

- Microwave on high 1 to 1½ minutes or until melted and smooth, stirring every 20 seconds.

- Dip the top of each marshmallow in the melted chocolate.

- Next, turn top side up and let stand for about 45 minutes or until set.

- Makes 24 cups.

- ENJOY

CONCLUSION

I hope you enjoyed the book as well as making and devouring these bomb cannabutterlicious edibles (and getting hella faded in the process!). I know I always do! Don't hesitate to make a bunch more and share them with your 420-friendly friends and family members. If you are still hungry for more mind-blowing THC-laced treats, keep an eye out for new upcoming titles from the Kief Preston's Time-Tested Edibles Cookbook Series, available in the Amazon Kindle store. For an updated list of available as well as upcoming titles, and to receive *Kief Preston's Time-Tested Edibles Cookbook: Coconut Edition* for FREE today, just go KiefPreston.com. And if you happen to be a hip-hop-head and you want something to vibe to while you're making or enjoying these incredible tasty edibles, I recommend that you visit KiefPreston.com to download your complimentary copy of the song "We Stay Smokin' On It" produced by me featuring Arizona rapper Mr. Go Hard.

"TAKE ACTION TODAY to help legalize weed

tomorrow!" -Kief Preston

THE KIEF PRESTON'S TIME TESTED EDIBLES COOKBOOK SERIES

Kief Preston's Time-Tested Edibles Cookbook: Medical

Marijuana Recipes

CANNABUTTER EDITION

Kief Preston's Time-Tested FASTEST Edibles Cookbook:

Quick Medical Marijuana Recipes

Kief Preston's Time-Tested Edibles Cookbook: Medical

Marijuana Recipes

CANNABIS CANDY EDITION

Kief Preston's Time-Tested Edibles Cookbook: Medical

Marijuana Recipes

LOW-CARB EDITION

Kief Preston's Time-Tested Edibles Cookbook: Medical

Marijuana Recipes

COOKING WITH KIEF EDITION

Kief Preston's Time-Tested Edibles Cookbook: Medical

Marijuana Recipes

MUFFINS EDITION

Kief Preston's Time-Tested Edibles Cookbook: Medical

Marijuana Recipes

CANNABIS COOKIES EDITION

Kief Preston's Time-Tested Edibles Cookbook: Medical

Marijuana Recipes

HIGH HOLIDAYS EDITION

KiefPreston.com

BEFORE YOU GO

If you liked this book, would you be kind enough to leave a favorable review? Every review helps!

Thanks again for taking the time to download and read this book. I really do appreciate it.

Stay up,

Kief Preston

YOUR BONUS

If you are sick of being persecuted by law enforcement and the millions of misinformed members of society, stand up for cannabis and help make this the year stoners coast to coast will remember as the greatest year EVER! The year weed was legalized! To find out how easy it is to help with the LEGALIZE IT 2016 movement, visit my blog at KiefPreston.com.

Did I mention that I have a BONUS GIFT waiting for you for taking action today to help legalize weed? You will also receive a copy of *Kief Preston's Time-Tested Edibles Cookbook: Medical Marijuana Recipes COCONUT OIL Edition absolutely* FREE.

CLICK HERE

Would you like to get the most important marijuana-related news updates every week for free?

For fluff-free, 100% no bullshit weed news check out *Weekly Weed News w/ Kief Preston* on YouTube.com

DISCLAMER

The recipes found in this publication are intended for medical marijuana patients, who are permitted by law to consume marijuana and products containing cannabis derivatives, as well as all individuals and/or groups who reside in a location where the consumption of cannabis is legal. If you do not fall into at least one of these two categories, you can still enjoy the recipes, but please substitute regular butter for cannabutter. Kief Preston does not encourage the breaking of any law (allegedly).

Made in the USA
Middletown, DE
22 December 2016